AF673893

IS LIFE A CLIMB, OR A VOYAGE?

(TWO LIVES CAUGHT IN 45 POEMS)

BY

ADRIAN ROGERS

ISBN: 978-93-6354-473-4

First Edition: 2025
Rs. 200/-

Cyberwit.net
HIG 45 Kaushambi Kunj, Kalindipuram
Allahabad - 211011 (U.P.) India
http://www.cyberwit.net
Tel: +(91) 9415091004
E-mail: info@cyberwit.net

Printed at Repro India Limited.

Contents

Part 1—St. Patrick

FOOTSTEPS IN THE SAND

I am—before a conelike peak,
perfected
above a western sea
unforgiving
as a landscape of sloped
deflected
boulder strewn remnants, while I,
reflected
in the soul see wildness...clouds
massing,
the wind-song's into nation rising,
seeing flashes
of my early days in lance-like
dashes
flickering into awareness...

soft-running light on the sea
touching an alien shore, fetching
consciousness...

beige-yellow sand grains sharp-clear
beneath waters almost...

mirror-reflective under an ambient
dawn-glowing light,silently.

Enslaved once, I fled to Gaul sea-tossed,
in an old boat packed with wolf hounds
yet not lost to the land of my servitude.

Such a plenitude of vision catching me,
on this westerly wave-wild shore.

"Come over and help us, holy boy!"

I studied, prayed, wrestling like Jacob,
with the Angel of memory bonded...

RETURNING

...but now gazing reflectively,
upon the Glass Castle
and the emerald rainbow,

I stand again
after long centuries
before an Autumn-purpled peak
towards the western sea
for what…
a shadowing acolyte, a knowing
of Lent as more
than an ascetic pilgrimage
of age sand histories
storinga soul's treasures
beyond what anyone may seek
in a single lifetime?

So be it,
we will tread the path of silence,
into silence, hearing only,
voices of earth, air, water, fire,
and our own hearts.

THE NEW FIRE

Be deafness liberated by the eye,voicing silently,
the speaking heart within a vigilance of waiting
step by step…

tension mounting, my conscious responsiveness
a part of future sun chained from a dark past,
step by step…

along the road to Tara breaking stone-hard rejection's
last defence against illumination, shaking foundations,
step by step…

of ancient certainties, lettinga new fire challenge,
the entities of darkness with conscience, berating
step by step…

hesitancy, as I light anew fire on the Hill of Slane
defying the dark in splendour, signalling a release
step by step…

from the pain of feral dominance.*Death,be not proud,*
though somehave called thee so—because I am,
step by step…

of the future from the future! Beltane shall give place,
to Easter, edge-cold enmity to love, and debating,
step by step…

with Druids—synchronous in mutual regard,preparing
for the Dove descending beyond all terrors, tensile,
step by step…

waiting, watching,until under her shadowing descent
wing spread, by Sophia in the Spirit I prophesy,
step by step…

that light shall banish darkness and enmity find...
no homing.

THE DEER'S CRY

Be the New Fire
our challenge to Beltane,
an eternal
rather than temporal gain,
a new spring...

I bind unto myself today,
the strong name of the Trinity...!

as defying the dark, we sing,
fearless
of a High King's wrath,
marching through the night
seeing only—by starlight
a herd of grazing deer,
protected
by the 'Breastplate of the Trinity'
as night passes
and dawn's breakout
is a shakeout,
of the night's miasma,
light—green reflected
on the hill of Tara.

AT THE HEAD OF THE PATH...

I am cast upon a mountain-scape,
blue/grey,a purple-headed summit
sun-striking
rayed between clouds overpassing,
pace-distanced many a trope
my gaze sweeping
horizon-dominating ranges, rising,

broken-topped westerly,
towards the sea
blue flared
late summer cloud-tinged
under a chill wind sighing fitfully
amid tussocky grasses
uncompromising as boulders

landscaped like curving shoulders,
weathered
as the body and soul of ages,
resisting the self
and released from desiring,

a forty-day tryst inspiring
timely prayers of overlooking
pummelled
by landward elemental forces,
hyper-somatic beings at great heights
inveigling
body mind and spirit

on a path relentlessly inquisitorial,
my goal...
a transcendental interceding
for the world soul.

TARA

Late summer sun partners earth
and air, touching
the green land with a share
of light-mellowed shimmering
willow-bordered waterflow,
onward glimmering
a merging and emerging glow,
as on the march to Tara
poised between two firmaments
the waters above and below
I wonder…
may the fire of Spirit descend,
new meanings capture a trend
step by step, in the march of history?

"Come over and help us, holy boy!"

"I, Angel of Mercy am the Matronit,
bride, mother, crone,
one with all who walk alone,
for this land consummation
and promise
clarifying, by inward vision
the green hill of Tara near
yet distant, the incision into time
of enlightenment
so, cease not my brother,
but labour in the light
and you will be, among bright...
dragon stars a voice for your people,
at the end of days."

UNDER SWIFT CLOUDSCAPES

Fast moving cloudscapes are passers-by but I
passing by endure the stones of pain sacrificially,

momentously painted on time by blood on stone
and awareness to hone self-focussed impulses,

sentenced under cloud-blackened onslaughts,
heart contoured,fluctuating in thoughts hosting,

sky-racers known by rain-flailing powers loosed,
washing the mountain and bloodied footprints

hard driving a mockery of storm/wind elementals
or, as incense spirit-thinned yet unstoppable

between Michael and the Dragon cutting-off thc sun
bleakly rendered into revelation's soul/scourging

active seeing and renewing of a mind unbarred,
scarred but aware as, coming into light stands one,

with me like an equinoctial mystery of precession
summoning a shafting splendour, rending overcast

mind-shaped forms, illuminating an essential grace—
within the moment, an inward radiance timeless,

free from regression in the soul as time's signature
is cancelled by a door closing…

YEARS OF PILGRIMAGE—PART 1

Locked in a prophetic past,
the spirit of Jeremiah
was, in the hopefulness of
migration a Scythian,
yet also one
with wandering tribes, until
among Druids cast,
by sacred springs
waters fresh and salt
sun/sky haunted lakes
the Morning and Evening Star
teaching Star-Fire mysteries,
and in forested lodges
of hidden wisdom
singing eternally
the story of creation
learning and teaching
under green filtered light
or shadows out-branching...

secretive time's vast sculpting,
mountains, forests,
plains,waters above
and below the firmament
while I...uncontested
through years un-contestable
of pilgrimage ways
have perfected the circle of love.

AT THE POINT OF THE THUNDER

As the first drum-rolling echo thunders,
frozen consciousness
lightning flared blunders
in a lesser responsiveness
to percussive stone showers
sharpening, aware,
unshrinking, enduring what empowers
rain-bathed
and, thus baptised before a tumultuous
discordant ensemble
breaking free...

drawing me
along a cloud-shadowed path
thunder-clapped, light speared,
whitely absorbed into spirit formations
hearing between out-spanning crashes
amid black-whirlpooled
sweeping immaterial concentrations
lost voices echo-calling
worlds-weary sorrowing
searching for light.

Holy Archangel Michael
soul-summon,
from beyond a terror of soullessness
to where is neither variableness,
nor shadow of turning,
where light awaits

where,cloaking, scattering and wavelike,
dark-smothering unreason
is a lightning-flash,
floored, undulating, not burning,
enclosed or encompassing.

YEARS OF PILGRIMAGE—PART 2

Coruscating light's splintered rainbow
from disunion by water
seeks a reunion,
descending from the stars
unto the sun in waiting
one and synonymous
with a radiance white overcoming
a countering splendour,
empowering
through times daughter the foretelling
of night's oncoming
under the Dragon Constellation

as now, on this mountain
in the wake of thunder departing
when the wind dies
may time from my heart not sunder
the mysteries,
their inspiration
histories of nations fulfilling
and through long years of pilgrimage
my consecration, thus contesting,
the might of negation...

bound-back in a love,
empowered by the Dove.

LIGHT ON A STRAIGHT UPSLOPE

Sun between parted clouds casts light
on the path's straight-stretching upslope.

Today, I am—

after rain pilgrim-stationed stones bright
glitter, reflective as a mind grope…

old, young, and spirit/bodied seeking
inner meaning, but a blue peak
distantly summoning, is saying?

Dumb and bonded—

unpredictability appears as a meek
inherited reaction sprung from praying!

Aftermath and reason, are—

as winds buffet capriciously, dying...
gradually on a pearl/white/gilded height.

Could it be otherwise—

haunting a suggestively daunting call
endeavouring to be…hope shining white?

On Croagh Patrick maybe, as ankles
slip/twist wet on stone austerity will cope,

fortitude atone,
obliterate illusion for truth alone, and
when Shamrock and Word intone…

fine-tuning creation in the land of the Trinity.

ARMAGH

Armagh, my green hill
my resting place
where the illumined will
finds a space...

perceiving coal escences,
pasts and futures retrieving,
from a knowing
of the Grail hidden mysteries
receiving—
from those who came down
leaving
traces of luminous presences.

Armagh, my green hill
my resting place
where the illumined will
finds a space...

overlooking in the light
forest, pasture
and the flowing waters
mysteries in their essences
understood against nemesis,
through times and seasons
innumerable
where the will fuses senses
glimpsing
splendours beyond conceiving.

NOTHING BEYOND THE PATH

After a rainstorm's banishment
the sun, strong burning pearl/hazing
sheens a melding into white,
drying a watery glitter off stones…

yet failing to implement the rule of light.

Slow drifting cloudscapes returning
brightness to mist, sight limiting,
for those who fritter away hope,
sifting dry bones
in the valley of memory,
grey-veil adown-rolling into silence
as the wind dies...
and the goal in a pilgrim's mind tries,
tentatively
to image purpose, discover selfhood.

Beyond inflexibility's rising path
mountainsides fall away,
and a seeker may only speculate,
unable long to concentrate...on
haunting sanctities,
bonded to a way where nothing is,
but precipitous infinity
dropped into a whispering stillness,
birthing inevitability,
until a blue mountain hare

overruns the stony track,
from cloudscapeto cloudscape.

Who will dare stretch a self,
upon the rack
of a hoped-for illumined escape?

THE HOMEWARD ROAD—PART 1

I have restored...
the Sun-Wheel to the Cross
fusing
all things into one
coalescing
times and seasons in the 'now'
re-lighting a flame of knowing,

its light growing,
for those tending the flame
fulfilling
that day when first I stepped,
on this once alien shore
fanning
the fire of love
for them to take, soon faraway,
perhaps
to the world's far side
where the last stars touch the sea.

Along the homeward road
to Armagh,
on my green hill a watchfire
nightlong will goad,
old memories
through whispering forest ways
on green-glowing days,
or shadowed when the sun strays,
but always
to my heart's desire…

ELEMENTAL TEMPTATIONS

It is incumbent upon me,
to blood these stones, see
light brought down,
stumbling but to rise endure
a storm wind's whip on my body
as one who tries against all odds
to achieve illumination as the wind dies.

Smother-drenching rain
cleanses vision marred by pain,
teaches divided being at the assize—of
judgment, uses a savaging flood,
testing endurance
through hope-vested devotion
as westward voices sever wind from water.

O daughter of time
by an emerging Sun, secret rhyme,
unity, climbs relentless, obedience to vision,
in the cloud my blanketing shroud
of self-doubt…

(Death be not proud
though some have called thee so)

duel...steep challenging elemental forces
sensing a visceral intensity
of fearsome opposition

so, test me by a stinging hail, I who know,
and will not fail in a repetitive tale...of
insidious implication.

Fire be in the sky and hope a front
against fear. Let us proceed in peace.

THE HOMEWARD ROAD—PART 2

At the end of the road
will my life's work,
be memory's load,
conscience's goad

or just the sound of summer's end?

Years flowed,
as by night and day
I sought the mother lode,
the secret code

of enlightenment, that divine trend

elucidating, sun
moon, dazzling stars,
the bright run
of light on water, having begun,

with another season another reason,

transmitting the light
and at last
under night skies vast
beyond images black and white
in suspension
of the eternal moment

'now'...hearing the voice of my guide.

VILLANELLE—THE FINAL UPSLOPE

On the final stone-scarred upslope
beyond self-doubt's confessional
affirming hope's realization

encouraged by a shafting light,
defying fear's recessional
on the final stone-scarred upslope

seeing what radiance has done,
by testing in a splendour white
affirming hope's realization

as with passing time a clouding
doubtfulness, no longer shrouding,
on the final stone-scarred upslope

shadowing its consummation
in a splendid consecration
affirming hope's realization

is summit crowned by a strong sun,
glorious, triumphant, as One
on the final stone-scarred upslope
affirming hope's realization.

THE SUMMIT—EVOCATION

Encircle me O Divine Sun
I conceal but to reveal,
secrets of the Father
in kinship of spirit, of strength.

Time with me has begun,
to lay bare the truth, not steal
eternal mysteries but rather
display by time's gauge length,
breadth, height, the vastness
of creation...

summit swirling clouds
are shrouds pulled back,
unveiling the limitless scope
of earth, sea, sky-born glories
encircling birds in flight
wing-sweeping splendours
across the sun's light.

I have striven—
forty fasting days and nights
wrestling with angelic powers
unbinding the limits
of revealed knowledge.

Encircle me O Divine Sun
I have defied the Morrigan
of war and death,
the hooded crow of fate...

where the western sea, of late
aquamarine sings a life breath,
cast-about with green
white-sand-ringed islands, while I
at the table of The Dagda
partake of the chalice
of eternal wisdom.

THE SUMMIT—BINDING EARTH AND WATER

Mountain slopes fall swift away,
heather-purple stone-studded
north, south, east, west
distantly edged grey
into a sounding silence
wind-song bird-call haunting
reverberating
...summit encircling.

I bind to me the earth power,
green and growing things
tilled and wild lands
level plains, rising and falling,
mountain peaks, daunting
...swept swirling.

I bind to me the power of water,
shimmering daughter
of Time the Father, singing,
thundering
breaking onto rocks, calling
into earth's song
summoning mysteries.

Power is a reason,
a land, a people,
each passing season,
the Great Work,
a shield against the treason
of evil powers.

THE SUMMIT—BINDING AIR AND FIRE.

Summit outpacing
I bind to me the powers of air,
storm and wildness,
stinging, lashing ice-winds
of the North,
soft, rain-drenched westerlies,
hot-breathed desert winds,
coolness of temperate climes
…still pacing.

I bind to me the power of fire,
Vulcan's fire, infernal desire
igniting a devouring flame
yet also...
the soft-edged glow
of lamp, candle
heat and light of ritual, a name,
the light of elemental mastery.

Birds arcing, encircling me,
answer my call,
singing, earth-voicing, water
air, fire, serenading
the aspiring of nations
songs of day and night
leaving me
on the ebb tide of power
invoking one more mystery.

THE SECRET OF BINDING

Empowered by the Trinity
enclosing at its heart the Rose and Cross
red with the blood of ages
foreshadowing
despite memory's dross
infinite freedom from entropic stages

transfiguration ends, but I—
binding the power of all things into One
stand, by love's decree,
within the scope of history
infusing whatever has been done,
on earth for good or ill.

Clothed in a cope of light I am,
beginning, ending,
and all things in between
a power in splendour, so be it.

I am a voice crying in the wilderness...

a treasury of knowledge from above
descended into light wingspread, love.

THE DESCENT

I stand, still in the light,
backwashed by withdrawing power,
feeling no more
lashing embodiments of revelation
past/present interchanging,
...grey clouded, ranging,
drawn back—as the wind dies,
held in a trance of consecration,
light pulsed passing moments,
earth-singing
transfigured, circling.

A sunlit downslope
drooping below sharp peaks rising
falls...purple-hazed
into a slant-lit afternoon
enchaining senses poised,
as a mind tries to sift
the contents of vision, footsore
yet resolute
at the mountain's boulder strewn foot.

My fast completed,
victorious yet timelessly repeated
I gather past lives into...the
measureless instant
for a people of the future,
as a herald re-sent
chain-linking
in the Lodge of Ages.

THE MESSENGER AND THE MESSAGE

"Turn aside, Patrick!"

On the ebb tide of vision's
aspirational fire
and elemental power,
a mountain blue shadowed
above the western sea
is now beyond even
the scan-sweeping scope
of an eagle's eye,
and for the incision of desire
into the heart, the dower
of that mysterious fountain
accessed by love
I am free,
beyond the leaven
of temptation to be, in hope,
one with all who...touch
the wings of the Dove.

Miles be few between heart and home,
on this night lit by Dragon stars.
My camp set, silence has come
and peace should be, but
withdraws; why?
Night's breath whispers, yet try,
as I might no answer find I
to a sense of unease,

no haunting, yet tense, aware,
as softness night-speaks its intent.

"Turn aside, Patrick!

"Follow me…to where land meets water.
Obey me in this, and as my word is true,
to you will it be given to speak
for your people at the end of days."

PASSING

I have lived,
the chapters of a lifetime
written by love,
and beyond reason
the ineffable.

My time's season,
retrieved from bondage
and above all else
unaccountable
a smother-darkening pride,
is...words and deeds,
gathered into one,
in this place
where waterways meet,
and in shaping
the ritual dance of greeting
to that eternally descending
light beyond light.

Enough...!

Delusional evil challenging
this land
will encounter rough wisdom,
in things hidden
under earth, running waters
an overarching sky,

and with love
answering the call
as I pass on my way
in peace…

Part 2—Beyond the Barrier.

PREPARATION--—ONE MORE VENTURING

Unstated purpose in his eyes
takes rhythmic light,
sea and sky
into one movement's
reflexive touching
of past futures
in weathered wood,
a boat's sand-cushioned bow.

The sea calls
mind-stirring discontent
with static earth
and soon-to-be dropped sand,
reality grounded
beneath a gull's wing.

Visions of distance
wrestle salt-sharp wind,
wash over a mind alert
like waves
against a sloping beach
their undertow-like lure
turning touch to grip,
a long hull seaward thrust.

"Let the tide take her,
with dream-trapped Ulysses
towards the withdrawing hem
of sea and sky."

FROM THE BEACH

Under the wind-light
wave-light song
a boat hesitates,
across a shingle-slides
sand-stony progression
anticipating
the reflective hunger
of a long sea road.

Goad and goal one
a self-realized
conditioned to solitary sailing
balances...
to have or to be
over depths incalculable
beyond echo-sounding,
the unseen
below, and above
to cloud embattled heights
yet bound by natural law,
invoking primal elements
eternally sun/cloud conflicting
colour change and ice blink,
earthborn yet scanning widely,
spurning the Abyssal plunge
a state of overcoming
for ultimate
immeasurable calm
unfettered by becoming.

OVER THE SHALLOWS

A sea path beyond surface living
alienates,
separating by glass clear water
lives of sand slope
rough/smooth stone
weed, coral and anemone,
a kaleidoscopic red, green, yellow
multi-shaded half-lit montage
shot through with fish darting,
or sliding flat bellied
amid the blue-black lurk
of rock haunting
crawling crustaceans, enchanted...

Here we have no continuing city,
but we seek one which is to come,

where neither scorching heat
wind bite, spray sting
and wave buffeting
can counter the song lure,
or defer accepted destiny,
harrying...
to the world's edge
for enlightenment beyond
a bottomless waterfall
or Zenith-soaring leap
above dragon rumours,
a serpentine yet stirring,
soaring mindfulness.

GOING DEEPER

Sea/sun/surface
is splashed iridescently,
a fluctuating
impermanent wind cross
not yet a gale-sweep
masking untrodden deeps
below sun dance penetration.

Think not yet--in air and light
of whale song echoing
far sounding planet encircling
until swift booming resonant
migrant singers
ocean refreshing
sunlight sided wave-cutting
wind summoning
resound...in echo chambers,
of body and soul
imprinting
a countering image
of lightless depths
in fathomless darkness.

Beyond heedlessness
a 'Right of passage'
attunes...
against the black night
siren-cold call
for a sea-voiced 'raising'
Morning Star rising.

VOLUNTARY EXILE

Does a dark age, cresting the next wave
roll in remorselessly,
parodying a 'Morning Glory'
cloud flowing processional,
the Ogmius return
to stem its onset
turning back again from Erin
renouncing
the sacred Oak Grove?

A back is turned
from a shell scattered beach
retreating into memory,
windblown sun
kissing head and hair
scarce noticed,
voiced forewarnings
of elemental conflict
perpetually re-enacted
not yet heard
as light filters
the many-coloured life dance
in shallows ending
at the drop.

Encroaching
a band of darkness is deepening,
guarding mysteries
from intrusion's global scope
beyond surf-wave terrors.

DANCE NO. 1—SEA/SUN

Illusory circles
above and below
white light blue filtered,
atmospheric magic
staging the sea/sun dance
scattered gold,
flinging wide
spun leaping bird calls,
deflecting
human illusions
of wood, water,
breath and blood
answer wave born,
couple-seeking
surging leaps
above and below
light condensed
into pearl drop
diamond
and sun fire
responsive
to Antarctica's
wing born summons,
air veils penetrable
veiling beauty elusive
beyond senses
flesh enclosed,
yet to know
the wind-sleep dream.

DANCE NO. 2—WIND/BIRD DANCE SONG FORMATIONS

Their songs without choruses
are solitary odes
self-existent
windswept
into contrapuntal threads
woven across a sea, air,
light rondo fantasia
tossed
on a planet's breath
free floating over blue
bouncing off cloud banks
gliding...
or hovering becalmed
suspended
between sky roof,
and sea sun-flash reflecting
carrying
across vastness to all and one
waiting
on a world's exhalation
into sigh, hiss, wail or hum
unpredictable
peripheral to vision
implanted on consciousness,
backdropped
by yellow lengthening rays
slanting beam-like into setting.

SUNSET SARABANDE

A scarlet to crimson blaze's
sacred fire glory
spreads
over waves declining
wind sigh fading
as the flame unrolls
a carpet wise
slow ceremonial
dance into silence
the last bird call
a dying echo
last wing beat
an inaudible whisper
lost, in the soft slap
of water on wood
against small breezes.

A boat's hull floats free,
almost drifting
suspended
between light and dark
in the stately ritenuto
of a Sunset Sarabande
as if the world's first day
declining had called up,
a True West
power of progression's
lighted pathway
from the unreal
to the real.

STAR CALL

Orion commands the night,
his insignia
a three-star belt above
gold on black, matching
three pyramids below
aligned for Leo's vernal equinox
'First Time' heralding
the 'Sons of Horus',
a call echoing through
Creation's moment
of age-old silence
across the Great Year
summoning a past
returning to greet
a voyager in time
half conscious
of infinite mystery,
while the sacrificial balance
of a splayed Southern Cross
between sky and sea
is a momentary intuition
of the All.

A star-dazzling canopy
self-defines,
emerging from formless
against motionless dark
as the Moon rides up
to dispute
the Hunter's rule.

MOONLIGHT UNDER SAIL

Scatter-clustered islands
under moon white dreaming
suspended between layers,
of light cool radiance float
above and below
mirroring
a sail light reflecting,
moon and star dancing
dipping slightly,
saluting the elements
where is no haven,
past moon-swept islands
westward sailing, hearing
a night-dark ocean calling
beyond spellbound land
over moon-paled water
with wind so light,
seas so slight
wave-lift minimal,
slowly passing, passing on.

A watery reflective
star-bright horizon
draws him, along...a
glimmering moon-path
but...nothing will alter,
the set of a sail, no tack,
change of course,
for a 'passer-by'
passing...passing on.

THE WANDERING ALBATROSS

Struggle is always in the take-off,
but wind summoning
is undeniable,
like a ghostly grey/white glider's
perpetual haunting
of the Roaring Forties
one thousand miles from land
seeking no resting place
from a blue-white ice flash,
compromising
gale-smeared horizons
turning his course awhile
south away
towards the Barrier.

Aloofly magical, a spirit guide
leaves no return,
meeting the Voyager's tack
across gale-punching gusts
through punishing, freezing seas
and storm-swept ages,
shadowed
by a faraway roaming
always returning
wind-born presence's
shadowing seaways spirit
across wind-wracked wastes of time...

"I am you..."

STORM SURGE

Sea/sky merger
a solitary waverider
torn sail reefed
soars, against unknowable
vanished horizons.
The sea's ripped-off surface
lashes drooping clouds,
morphing running waves
into hills leaping
against falling skies
cyclonic fury
blending air and water
a seething union's
other state of being
the becoming,
of an undiscriminating entity
unstoppable
raising him
storm-battered
towards the centred eye
casting-through
transformative
spear-like,
balancing
beyond self-awareness
conquering
a symbolic encompassing
past-to-future flights,
exaltation
and overcoming.

THE ROCK

Sea power defies the hermetic dictum,
'As above so below'
frothed grey waves are both and neither,
growing, sinking,
steep-sided, diminishing.

A white shaft
rends a lowering cloud cover
focussing a column
darkly distant
yet paling under sun fingers
down-thrust through storm smother,
a rock
founded in the ocean bed
summoning a revelation.

A high-risen challenger
austerely terrible
defines, discriminates,
judges, above
below...a fused state
and the Rock,
a dreaded
repelling attraction
that navigators must pass
fearing its lodestone power
yet accepting the lurching
grey wave lour,
to reach the everlasting
'Sun-door at World's End.'

CLOUD-BORN—THE ALBATROSS AGAIN

A cloud—born
sun-winged wanderer
is last seen near the Barrier
above pink/white/blue
light-caught ice flashes
and minimal lifting
cold-gloomed seas,
a piercing light-spear
targets white wings on the turn
under clarifying skies
answering the call
of a rolling, depth-resonant ocean
northward unbroken
but for temporary island refuges
and the Rock.

Your other self
is bent sail passing an awesome
sheer white-sided form's
untouchably cloud touching beauty
and terror.

"Shadow-guide the Voyager
beyond storm and calm
mediating light, air,
sea-echo and bird call
spray-scattering wonders
of life forms risen from deep places
linked...
until you reach, the Great Silence."

PASSING

The Rock magnetizes---
positive/negative
siren and harpy
smooth-faced
forbidding,
presiding over long rollers
diminishing,
no longer foamed or steep sided,
storm-clouds breaking up,
against a blue
sun-bursting backdrop.

The Rock is abeam to port,
and full-sail hoist
reflects an onward urge
as the boat heels
not quite gunwale under,
occasionally veering gusts
swing wildly the boom,
but the Master, sea-wise,
no lee-shore fearing
knows his sun-tracked course as true,
with feet braced against pitch and roll
sky-gazing briefly,
seeing again
a wind-riding ghostly wanderer
surfing the high airs
a kindred spirit returning,
to the Voyager's recognition,
a state of being, no longer alone.

BECALMED

Between clockwise
counterclockwise
current and wind flows
airless inertia like cool doldrums
flattens the sea,
sails hang motionless,
a boat's hull mirrored,
her lengthening shadow
stretched across the surface.

How many blood-fire sunsets
will flame path
unresponsive watery expanses,
how many expectations
hang dead...?

Floating above darkness
between the fathomless
and uncharted
is a hovering,
intuited fear of things hidden.

Half believing, he waits...for
what might or might not rise
while a ghost-white familiar
glides overhead,
until a mood-swinging breeze
transcends unreality's irrational,
haunting invasion,
...an awakening.

CATCHING WINDSONG

A light breeze creases the sea's surface,
an outward breath
sighed into stillness,
sails snap
rigging creaks
water softly slaps the boat's hull,
hope echoes
returning bird calls
a flurry of arcing patterns,
moving airs infiltrate.

A soft wind-song
out-filters haze
cleaning light
veiled yellow to reflective white,
hesitantly
the boat catches wind spun voices
answering a quickening breeze

...the voyage resumes.

ICE BLINK

The sky's all over pale
concave neutrality
refines light
cooled white by distant ice breath.

Almost silence
leaves a fine breeze humming,
and delicately blue/white flashes
coming and going like eye-blinks
finger the sky,
as mystery from beyond the Barrier
reaches out,
enfolding a voyager sailing
a dreamed fulfillment
into lengthening light.

LENGTHENING LIGHT

Towards the Barrier
lengthening whitening light
crystallizes
a long-imagined world
cool but grey-cold no longer
beyond the ice blink.

Far down translucent depth
and blue pearl cloudless sky
shimmers,
a layered radiance
water-pale gold/white
for eyes enlightened
gazing into the beyond
above and below.

From stormbound
darkly shadowed worlds
he floats free,
in windless air still drawn
inward and higher,
an ending of beginnings
where deeps rise
revealing red/green
outspread untrodden forests
in shallower seas reflecting
life reversed, mirrored,
known of but unspoken

by a ghost/white sky companion
whose every glance
turns outward from within
as the veiling form
of everything
where the Barrier rises
whitely mist-like, endlessly
beyond...all things.

THE SINGING

Stars no longer heaven bound,
descend...
through lengthening light
seaward into song.
Fiery comet-tailed
white falling spectaculars
leaving the macrocosm
race down...
before the curtaining Barrier
released from wandering
in the Great Year's wheel
flame-bending into forms
unseen on earth
yet summoning earth voices
calling the last temptation into song,
a white voiced calling
sine toned breathing,
pan flute-like chanting,
running notes
into long serpentine melismas

turn back,
from the unknown
beyond known things
turn back,
to heat, cold, cool thinking, hot desire,
turn back,
from lilies in a shrinking sea
turn...into the fading...turn...

THE LAST TEMPTATION

From waterline-burned vessels of past lives
the Voyager has turned,
from shipwrecks, shoreline strandings,
storm, calm, fire and ice
night terror and alarm,
from landings on strange beaches,
from hilltop ruins of unrealized hopes
soundboards
for whistling snow-flurried winter winds,
from loves
desired familiar things
passion fires sunk to smouldering ash,
he has turned.

The last flame dies,
he has turned,
from chanted mysteries
runes of power
the broken staff,
Prospero's cast-off-book of magic mastery.

The sirens say,
'Turn back,
do not forsake the known
for the abyss of imponderable things,
retrieve your sun and moon
from the dustbin of unrealized dreams,
turn back.'

A muffled grating scratches the silence,
keel sand-grounded in a sea of lilies
not far beneath his feet,
time is...
a letting-go,
no turning back
matter is...
finally renounced.

BEYOND THE BARRIER

Water now sweet is almost light
for a passing into endless dawn's
'Sun-door at World's End',
a condition of unconcern
with possessing.

He will not see again the falling leaf
the dying fire
time ebbing like the tide,
feet touch sand cool and lilies white
spread round his boat
carpeting
from centre to horizon.

Bells no longer chime the regulated hours,
old songs beyond hearing
cannot recall One long passed on
with empty hands,
his grounded boat unmoored,
beautifully unnecessary
sails idle, rigging slack,
unworn in timelessness.

New songs will draw him in
unheard
before his passing through
leaving one world as he entered it,
alone...
in mist-white shining

arising before the entrance
beyond looking back
for the unknowing
as veil-soft radiance
clouds a passing, until lifted…

beyond The Barrier.

www.ingramcontent.com/pod-product-compliance
Ingram Content Group UK Ltd.
Pitfield, Milton Keynes, MK11 3LW, UK
UKHW041316190726
13845UKWH00025B/305

9 789363 544734